77 Ways to Be a Father after the Separation

Written by Dr. Jake Golden, IV

This book is dedicated to my Princess Caylah Simone. I pray that I can be as great a father to you as my father was to me. I pray that I can be someone you look up to, someone you imitate, someone you respect… a great father and dad. I love you more than myself.

Love Daddy

no. 1.

Pay Your Child Support.

no. 2.

Set up

visitation

with **your**

children.

no. 3.

Visit

consistently.

no. 4.

Compliment your **children** often.

no. 5.

Hug them **often** as possible.

no. 6.

Kiss them

often.

no. 7.

Tell them that you love them often.

no. 8.

Always buy gifts on holidays.

no. 9.

Write your kids letters.

no. 10.

Take your daughter on dates.

no. 11.

Hug and kiss your son.

no. 12.

Teach your son to hold the door for women.

no. 13.

Teach your kids to change a tire.

no. 14.

Treat the mother with the utmost respect no matter how you feel.

no. 15.

Smile often.

no. 16.

Watch movies with your kids.

no. 17.

Visit your child's school at least once per month.

no. 18.

Buy your children's teacher gifts on holidays.

no. 19.

Place a lot of emphasis on education.

no. 20.

Have an opinion about world issues.

no. 21.

Teach your children to wash a car.

no. 22.

Cry with
them.

no. 23.

Give great advice on friendships.

no. 24.

Teach your son to cut grass.

no. 25.

Teach your son to tie a Windsor Knot.

no. 26.

Listen to your children.

no. 27.

Ride in the car with them without the radio.

no. 28.

Respect their opinions.

no. 29.

Play video games with them.

no. 30.

Sit in the dark with them.

no. 31.

Take your kids to your workplace.

no. 32.

Don't miss a ball game they are participating in.

no. 33.

Always laugh
at their jokes.

no. 34.

Always keep their gifts.

no. 35.

Always be nice but firm.

no. 36.

Always act in character towards them.

no. 37.

Let your guard down every now and then.

no. 38.

Say I am sorry when you make a mistake.

no. 39.

Be yourself.

no. 40.

Let them play with your toys.

no. 41.

Always answer your cell phone when they call.

no. 42.

Always reply to their texts.

no. 43.

Say yes often
and no when
necessary.

no. 44.

Read them a
book even
when they
are older.

no. 45.

Sleep on the floor with them.

no. 46.

Take them on a camping trip even if you are afraid of bugs.

no. 47.

Make up a story and tell them.

no. 48.

Always be strong and faithful.

no. 49.

Show them
integrity and
character.

no. 50.

Don't use vulgar language ever!

no. 51.

Teach your daughter to respect herself.

no. 52.

Tell your daughter that she is beautiful.

no. 53.

Send your daughter flowers just because.

no. 54.

Don't hurt your children.

no. 55.

Respect the mom's new boyfriend.

no. 56.

Don't cause drama with your Ex.

no. 57.

Love God!

no. 58.

Take your kids to church with you.

no. 59.

Learn to do your daughter's hair.

no. 60.

Understand that your children are changing and respect it.

no. 61.

Acknowledge your kid's accomplishm ents.

no. 62.

Remember their stories.

no. 63.

Listen to the music they listen to… So you know.

no. 64.

Teach them forgiveness.

no. 65.

Teach them about sex.

no. 66.

Teach them how to love others.

no. 67.

Always be on time for their programs.

no. 68.

Remember their best friend's name.

no. 69.

Teach your kids how to date.

no. 70.

Don't laugh at your kids when they make a mistake.

no. 71.

Always provide for them.

no. 72.

Share your food with them.

no. 73.

Teach them to believe in dreams, Santa Claus, the Tooth Fairy, and the Easter Bunny.

no. 74.

Teach them
to love God.

no. 75.

Teach them how to play by the rules.

no. 76.

Talk to them on the phone.

no. 77.

Always be a great DAD!